P9-EAI-921

THE PORTABLE **7** HABITS™

Choice

Choosing the Proactive Life You Want to Live

THE **7** HABITS
OF HIGHLY EFFECTIVE PEOPLE ®

Other Portable 7 Habits Books
Vision: Defining Your Destiny in Life
Purpose: Focusing on What Matters Most
Abundance: Fulfilling Your Potential for Success
Trust: Sharing Ideas, Insights, and Understanding
Synergy: Connecting to the Power of Cooperation
Renewal: Nourishing Body, Mind, Heart, and Soul

Other Books from Franklin Covey

The 7 Habits of Highly Effective People
The 7 Habits of Highly Effective Families
The 7 Habits of Highly Effective Teens
The 7 Habits of Highly Effective Teens Journal
Daily Reflections for Highly Effective Teens
Daily Reflections for Highly Effective People
Living the 7 Habits

Loving Reminders for Kids
Loving Reminders for Couples
Loving Reminders for Families
Loving Reminders Teen to Teen
Loving Reminders to Make Kids Laugh
Quotes and Quips

Franklin Covey
2200 West Parkway Boulevard
Salt Lake City, Utah 84119-2099

Concept: Cheryl Kerzner
Design: Jenny Peterson
Illustration: Tammy Smith
Editing: Sunny Larson, Debra Harris, Lynn Frost, Lyn Christian, Reid Later, Crickett Willardsen, Matthew Clyde, Judy Ball, Todd Davis, Holli Karren, Donelle Deinstadt, Shelley Orgill

Manufactured in United States of America

ISBN 1-929494-02-5

CONTENTS

AUTHENTICITY 3

CHANGE 17

CHOICE 27

COURAGE 41

CREATIVITY 53

DETERMINATION 65

INITIATIVE 75

INTEGRITY 85

RESPONSIBILITY 95

SUCCESS 105

Life is a book and you are its author. You determine its plot and pace

and you—only you—turn its pages.

—BETH MENDE CONNY

INTRODUCTION

Your life is not just happening around you. Whether you know it or not, it is carefully designed by you. Or carelessly designed by you. It is, after all, your choice. You choose happiness. You choose sadness. You choose decisiveness. You choose ambivalence. You choose success. You choose failure. You choose courage. You choose fear. Just remember that every moment, every situation provides a new choice. And in doing so, gives you a perfect opportunity to do things differently to produce more positive results.

In The Portable 7 Habits series, we've simplified the powerful principles behind *The 7 Habits of Highly Effective People* by Stephen R. Covey to fit in with your busy life. (Of course, should you be the one person in the entire universe who hasn't read the original book, please be our guest and pick one up to get the big picture.)

With *Choice: Choosing the Proactive Life You Want to Live* there are no roadmaps to follow. No instructions. No how-tos. And no formulas for success. Instead you'll find a collection of questions, inspirational quotes, short stories, and anecdotes designed to help you deal with the challenges you face every day. And to help you make the best possible choices.

As you turn these pages, take the words of advice to heart, mind, and soul. Think about what you read. Ponder how and what it would take to incorporate change in your life. Let the wisdom inspire you to take initiative. Learn, grow, and create new options. Empower yourself. Take responsibility. Influence your circumstances rather than be a victim to them. Shape your future rather than be shaped by it. Choose to control rather than be controlled. Be the author of your own life rather than allowing someone else to write it for you.

In essence, make it a habit to be proactive.

HABIT 1: BE PROACTIVE®

Take responsibility for your life.

AUTHENTICITY

Until we know ourselves and are aware of ourselves as separate from others and from the environment—until we can be separated even from ourselves so that we can observe our own tendencies, thoughts, and desires—we have no foundation from which to know and respect other people, let alone to create change within ourselves.

—STEPHEN R. COVEY, *The 7 Habits of Highly Effective Families*

Let
the world
know you as you are, not as you think you should be—because sooner or later, if you are posing, you will forget the pose and then where are you?

—FANNY BRICE

When I meet people or get in a new relationship,

I start putting all these repressive restrictions on myself;

I can't have my feelings.

Can't have my wants and needs.

Can't have my history.

Can't do the things I want,

feel the feelings I'm feeling,

or say what I need to say.

I turn into this repressed,

perfectionistic robot,

instead of being who I am: ME!

—UNKNOWN

Give yourself permission to be who you are.

Regardless of whether that "who" is deeply attached to outlet malls on a cellular level, dots an "i" with a heart, or has a lifelong dream to become an insurance adjuster.

Everything was going so well. She hadn't seen any flaws in me. Now she sees a side.

What side?

A bad side, an ugly side.

Oh, so what?

So what? I wasn't planning on showing that side for another six months. Now you made me throw off the whole learning curve.

—JERRY AND GEORGE, *SEINFELD*

Follow your heart.

Any other path leads to
someone else's dream.

Do you remember the first time you stood up for something you believed in, despite the fact that you stood alone?

When was it?

What happened?

Before we can care for others, we must learn to

LOVE THE SELF.

This is true, as well, for another reason: Without self-acceptance, we're like empty vessels always seeking to be filled from another's cup. Even when we do good, there will be a hidden agenda based more on getting than on giving—"see how good I am, think well of me, love me please." Yet no approval seems quite enough to fill the cup. It's always leaking from a hole in the center. Healthy self-regard plugs that hole and fills us from within.

—DREW LEDER

When a child loves you for a long, long time—
REALLY loves you,
then you become Real.
Generally, by the time you are real,
most of your hair has been loved off,
and your eyes drop out
and you get loose in the joints
and very shabby.
But these things don't matter at all,
because once you are real,
you can't be ugly,
except to people who
don't understand.

—MARGERY WILLIAMS

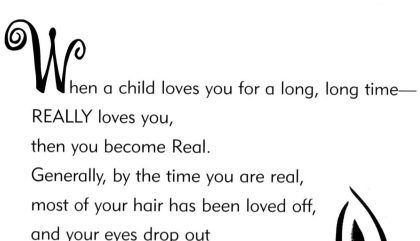

Do you appreciate your uniqueness? Can you sort yourself out from others in a crowd? Try asking those you trust for insights about your uniqueness. Seek feedback from peers at work as well as peers in your personal life.

Go on a hunt for your uniqueness.

Frank Lloyd Wright said,
"If architecture is what I conceive it to be, there has never
been another architect."

What are you?

What do you conceive?

What you resist, persists.

Your truth will find you no matter where you hide. Ignoring your inner voice or closing yourself off to your inner truth only invites it to show up in other, more negative ways, such as depression, addictive behaviors, or simply discontent. The sooner you open to your truth, the quicker and farther you can advance along your path. Life flows more smoothly when we heed our inner message.

If you
can't be
yourself,
who else can you be?

AND WHY
WOULD YOU
WANT TO?

We do not believe in ourselves until someone reveals that deep inside us something is valuable, worth listening to, worthy of our trust, sacred to our touch. Once we believe in ourselves we risk curiosity, wonder, spontaneous delight or any experience that reveals the

human spirit.

—e. e. cummings

CHANGE

Proactive people focus their efforts in the Circle of Influence. They work on the things they can do something about. The nature of their energy is positive, enlarging and magnifying, causing their Circle of Influence to increase.

—STEPHEN R. COVEY, *The 7 Habits of Highly Effective People*

To exist is to change,

to change is to mature,

to mature is to go on

creating oneself endlessly.

—HENRY BERGSON

Learn anything new lately?

19

Live out of your

IMAGINATION

not your history.

—STEPHEN R. COVEY

Pack a lunch, enjoy

the trip and quit asking

if you're there yet.

You'll know when

you've arrived.

When people make changes in their lives in a certain area, they may start by changing the way they talk about that subject, how they act about it, their attitude toward it, or an underlying decision concerning it.

—JEAN ILLSLEY CLARKE

Focus

on what you are moving
toward rather than what you
are leaving behind.

—ALAN COHEN

There is no such thing as a problem
without a gift for you in its hands.

**You seek
problems
because
you need
their gifts.**

—RICHARD BACH

Change brings opportunities

when people have been planning for it, are ready for it, and have just the thing in mind to do when the new state comes into being.

—ROSABETH MOSS KANTER

25

Do you have your own set of happy words?

Sometimes a good word can make tough changes easier. Try using, "I am facing this challenge," in place of "I have this problem."

CHOICE

Habit 1 embodies the greatest gift that we as humans uniquely have: the power to choose. Next to life itself, is there a greater gift? The truth is that the basic solutions to our problems lie within us. We can't escape the nature of things. Like it or not—realize it or not—principles and conscience are within us.

——STEPHEN R. COVEY, *The 7 Habits of Highly Effective Families*

Where are your choices taking your life?

All men and women are born, live, suffer, and die: what distinguishes us one from another is our dreams, whether they be dreams about worldly or unworldly things, and what we do to make them come about. We do not choose to be born. We do not choose our parents. We do not choose our historical epoch, the country of birth, or the immediate circumstances of our upbringing. We do not, most of us, choose to die; nor do we choose the time and conditions of our death. But within the realm of choicelessness, **we do choose how we live.**

—JOSEPH EPSTEIN

Many of us have been programmed to believe that we do not have the power to choose what we want in our lives. We do. Some of us think we cannot move beyond prescribed limits, constraints, and restrictions placed upon us by others. We can. It is often difficult to see the bright side of a difficult situation. It is difficult, not impossible. We are powerful enough to move beyond limits in order to do the impossible, when we choose to. But we have to make the choice. The law of cause and effect is a fact of life, which turns our choices into a reality. Every thought we have leads to a choice. Every word we speak supports our choices we make. Every action we take is a choice today, which has implications on our tomorrow, next week, and next year. Nothing is impossible tomorrow when we take the time to choose, today. Today, choose to be courageous, rather than fearful. No matter what you face, choose clarity over confusion. Remember to choose discipline over habit; when things are at their worst and when you are at your lowest, choose love over hate or anger.

Choices

cause a mighty vibration which in effect brings back to us more of what we give out.

—IYANLA VANZANT

Become a CSO.

(Chief Selection Officer of your own life!)

If you don't take control of your life, don't complain when others do.

—BETH MENDE CONNY

A peacefulness follows any decision, even the wrong one.

—RITA MAE BROWN

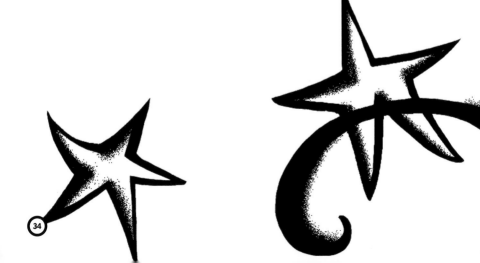

People have more options than they think they do.

But most people spend more time planning their vacations than thinking about what they want to do with their lives.

—BOB MCDONALD

The Samurai

In Japan, there is a story of a samurai who is being chased by a bear. He runs off a cliff. As he's falling, he grabs a branch. He looks up and sees the bear leaning over the cliff, clawing at his head, missing only by inches. As he looks down to the ground, only about fifteen feet below, he sees a lion leaping up, missing his feet only by inches. As he looks at the branch he is clutching, he sees two groundhogs gnawing away at it. He watches as his lifeline disappears, bite by bite. As he takes a deep, long breath, he notices next to his branch a clump of wild strawberries. In the midst of the clump is a great, red, juicy strawberry. With his one free hand, he reaches over, picks the strawberry, puts it in his mouth, chews it slowly, and says, "Ah—delicious."

—THOMAS F. CRUM

Do you enjoy the good fortune of eating a delicious strawberry or worry about the lion biting at your heels?

Do not wait for
ideal circumstances;
they never come.
—JANET ERSKINE STUART

37

EVERY MOMENT OF EVERY DAY, CHOOSE.

Choose to do the right thing, the tough thing—not the familiar easy thing. Choose the way of the warrior or the way of the coward. Make your choice out of love instead of fear. Choose from the heart. Choose to live fully, not to sleepwalk through your life. Choose to respond with the way you really feel, not the way you're supposed to feel. Choose the mineral water over the soda; choose the lemon

juice and olive oil over the blue cheese; choose the walk in the park over the ride to the mall. Choose simplicity over extravagance. Choose conversation over the television. Choose to talk things out rather than stew in your anger overnight. Choose compassion and generosity. Choose to smile instead of frown. Make your own choices in your own time and choose to stick with them.

— RACHEL SNYDER

When we die and go to Heaven, our Maker is not going to say: "Why didn't you discover the cure for such and such?" The only thing we're going to be asked at that precious moment is

"Why didn't you become you?"

—ELIE WEISEL

COURAGE

Proactive people are still influenced by external stimuli, whether physical, social, or psychological. But their response to the stimuli, conscious or unconscious, is a value-based choice or response. As Eleanor Roosevelt observed, "No on can hurt you without your consent." In the words of Gandhi, "They cannot take away our self respect if we do not give it to them." It is our willing permission, our consent to what happens to us, that hurts us far more than what happens to us in the first place.

—STEPHEN R. COVEY, *The 7 Habits of Highly Effective People*

While you're struggling with the fear that it can't be done, somebody else is doing it.

—HOLLY STIEL

Ella Fitzgerald dreamed of being a doctor until she happened to hear about Amateur Night at Harlem's famed Apollo Theatre. She decided to participate and planned her dance routine. As soon as she got on stage, her legs froze. The audience laughed at her awkward deer-in-the-headlights stance. In order to distract them, she began to sing songs she had memorized from her mother's records. The audience was quickly silenced—awestruck with her talent. She went on to win a $25 prize and launch a magnificent singing career.

Risk!

Risk anything!

Care no more for the opinions of others, for those voices. Do the hardest thing on earth for you. Act for yourself. Face the truth.

—KATHERINE MANSFIELD

Are you sleepwalking through your life?

$\mathcal{D}$on't be frustrated by your own inexperience. All green things grow and blossom eventually with enough nurturing.

If you have to swallow a toad,
don't stare at it too long.

—CONNIE HILLIARD

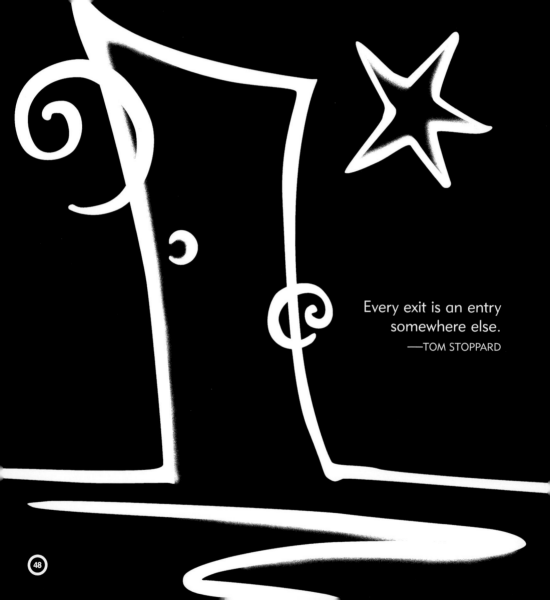

Every exit is an entry
somewhere else.
—TOM STOPPARD

What's the worst thing that could happen if you faced your fear?

Well, the best thing that could happen is that you could conquer

your fear. You could accomplish what you thought you couldn't

accomplish. You could become wildly happy and successful. And

you could like it. Imagine how good you would feel to be free of

burden. To feel strong and capable. Now, is your answer to the

first question going to keep you from all that?

IT

takes courage to uncover your pain
and to touch all of your feelings with
compassion. But it is one of the most
important habits you'll ever learn.

—SUSAN SANTUCCI

What would it take to get out of your

comfort
zone?

got courage?

CREATIVITY

Within the freedom to choose are those endowments that make us uniquely human. In addition to self-awareness, we have imagination—the ability to create in our minds beyond our present reality. We have conscience—a deep inner awareness of right and wrong, of the principles that govern our behavior, and a sense of the degree to which our thoughts and actions are in harmony with them. And we have independent will—the ability to act based on our self-awareness, free of all other influences.

—STEPHEN R. COVEY, *The 7 Habits of Highly Effective People*

I always paint my own reality.

—FRIDA KAHLO

Take a ride on your own creativity bus.

Make your own rules. Your own reality.

Go where your vision takes you.

Defy convention.

Unleash the creative dog

that's barking to get out.

I don't want life to imitate art.

I want life to be art.

—CARRIE FISHER

If you could develop a new talent, what would it be?

*F*ashion entered the twentieth century with Coco Chanel. She did to the fashion world what Ford did to industry, Picasso to art, Stravinsky to music, Woolf to literature: she rebelled against the old rules and formulas to create a new, definitive style that other designers, no matter how unique themselves, would incorporate in one form or another. Chanel's approach to fashion reflected a vision of life in general: "I invented my life by taking for granted that everything I did not like would have an opposite, which I would like. Fashion is not simply a matter of clothes. Fashion is in the air, born upon the wind. One intuits it. It is in the sky and on the road."

What could be?

Begin here.

Who said you can't

color outside the lines?

Most of us have forgotten how to play,

forgotten the **joy of creativity.**

Without joy, we run from pain.

Without creativity, we run from emptiness.

The faster we run, the more severe our addictions.

We cannot face our nothingness,

the ultimate anguish of

living a life knowing who we are not,

not who we are.

—MARION WOODMAN

A picture?

A policy?

What do you want

merry?

A sweater?

music?

A discovery?

A garden?

believe?

to make?

A cake?

friends?

A date?

A move?

A deal?

What would it be like
if we lived our lives
as works of art in progress?

If each breath and each action were part of an unfolding masterpiece?

If we saw the shadows and the light areas as part of the composition?

Accepted it all? Found joy in the beauty of it?

DETERMINATION

We can make a promise—and keep it. Or we can set a goal—and work to achieve it. As we make and keep commitments, even small commitments, we begin to establish an inner integrity that gives us the awareness of self-control and the courage and strength to accept more of the responsibility for our own lives.

—STEPHEN R. COVEY, *The 7 Habits of Highly Effective Families*

I have to remember to tell the negative committee
that meets in my head to

sit down
and shut up.

—KATHY KENDALL

When you plant a seed, don't continually dig up the soil to see how the roots are doing. With patience and determination your dreams will come to fruition.

If you can't

go through it

to get out of it,

go around.

I have met many wanna-bes.

I distinguish the wannas from the gonnas because the wanna-bes all think someone else is to blame for their problems—By contrast, gonna-bes say:

"What?
There's no door here?
I'll build one."

—K. CALLAN

Find out what you love.
Do it because you love it.
Stick with it.
Start now.

—BARBARA SHER

Reach high,
for stars lie hidden in
your soul.
Dream deep,
for every dream precedes
the goal.

——PAMELA VAULL STARR

Ever try to put the skids on an ant? It's virtually impossible. They never stop. Put one to the test some day. Pretend you're five years old again, and make a little hill in an ant's path. The ant will walk up and over the top without braking. It will go into a hole, over a log, through grass. If it can't go through, it will go around. An ant will never turn around and walk the other way, no matter what obstacles are in its path.

Try applying that kind of tenacity to your life. Of course, you'll want to use your brain too. But in the determination department, be an ant. Refuse to be stopped. Keep going, and learn as you go. People who patiently persist finally see their dreams come true.

If you're not deciding for yourself, who is?

The quality of our life isn't determined by what we encounter in a lifetime. It is determined by **how we encounter life.**

INITIATIVE

As you study the other six habits, you will see that each depends on the development of your proactive muscles. Each puts the responsibility on you to act. If you wait to be acted upon, you will be acted upon. And growth and opportunity consequences attend either road.

——STEPHEN R. COVEY, *The 7 Habits of Highly Effective People*

If you're never scared or embarrassed or hurt, it means you never take any chances.

—JULIA SOREL

*L*ife is truly a ride. We're all strapped in and no one can stop it. When the doctor slaps your behind, he's ripping your ticket and away you go. As you make each passage from youth to adulthood to maturity, sometimes you put your arms up and scream, sometimes you just hang on to that bar in front of you. But the ride is the thing. I think the most you can hope for at the end of life is that your hair's messed, you're out of breath and you didn't throw up.

—JERRY SEINFELD

It isn't a calamity to die with dreams unfulfilled, but it is a calamity not to dream...It is not a disgrace not to reach the stars, but

it is a disgrace to have no stars to reach.

—BENJAMIN MAYS

bad habit may give you temporary pleasure. But in the end, it creates more misery than it's worth.

What bad habit would you like to get rid of once and for all?

My parents always told me

I could
do anything

but never told me how long it would take.

—RITA RUDNER

Curiosity killed the cat.

It also helped Stephen Hawking formulate a stunning theory on the origin and fate of the universe.

It helped Bill Gates give birth to a software empire.

It helped Maria Montesorri revolutionize early childhood education.

It helped Jacques Cousteau make scuba diving a possibility for the everyday joe.

It helped Martha Graham catapult the world of dance into a new century.

What are you curious about?

You have control over three things

- what you think
- what you say
- and how you behave

To make a change in your life, you must recognize these gifts are the most powerful tools you possess in shaping the form of your life.

—SONYA FRIEDMAN

If you **risk nothing** then you

risk everything.

—GEENA DAVIS

What would you do if you **could?**

What could you do if you **would?**

INTEGRITY

We have all known individuals in very difficult circumstances, perhaps with a terminal illness or a severe physical handicap who maintain magnificent emotional strength. How inspired we are by their integrity! Nothing has a greater, longer lasting impression upon another person than the awareness that someone has transcended suffering, has transcended circumstance, and is embodying and expressing a value that inspires and ennobles and lifts life.

—STEPHEN R. COVEY, *The 7 Habits of Highly Effective People*

If you were in charge, what would you change?

People are unreasonable, illogical and self-centered. Love them anyway. If you do good, people will accuse you of selfish, ulterior motives. Do good anyway. If you are successful, you will win false friends and true enemies. Succeed anyway. The good you do today will be forgotten tomorrow. Do good anyway. Honesty and frankness make you vulnerable. Be honest anyway. The biggest person with the biggest ideas can be shot down by the smallest person with the smallest mind. Think big anyway. What you spend years building may be destroyed overnight. Build anyway. People really need help but may attack if you help them. Help people anyway. Give the world the best you have and you might get kicked in the teeth.

Give the world the best you've got anyway.

—UNKNOWN

People are like
stained-glass windows.

They sparkle and shine when the sun is out but when darkness sets in, their true beauty is revealed only if there is a light from within.

—ELIZABETH KUBLER-ROSS

Keep my words positive:

Words become my behaviors.

Keep my behaviors positive:

Behaviors become my habits.

Keep my habits positive:

Habits become my values.

Keep my values positive:

Values become my destiny.

There is no dress rehearsal:

This is one day in your life.

——MOHANDAS K. GANDHI

The mind gives you
thousands of ways
to say no,
but there's only
one way to say yes,
and that's from
the heart.

—SUZE ORMAN

Trust

is the highest form of human motivation.

—STEPHEN R. COVEY

Integrity is not a 90 percent thing,

not a 95 percent thing; either you have it or you don't.

—PETER SCOTESE

SHOW UP

and participate.

There will be a test later.

We join spokes together in a wheel,

but it is the center hole that makes it move.

We shape clay into a pot,

but it is the emptiness inside that holds whatever we want.

We hammer wood for a house

but it is the inner space that makes it livable.

We work with being

but non-being is what we use.

—LAO-TZU

RESPONSIBILITY

We are responsible for our own effectiveness, for our own happiness, and ultimately, I would say, for most of our circumstances…Knowing that we are responsible—"response-able"—is fundamental to effectiveness and to every other habit of effectiveness.

—STEPHEN R. COVEY, *The 7 Habits of Highly Effective People*

When I stand before God at the end of my life, I would hope that I would not have a single bit of talent left and could say, "I used everything you gave me."

—ERMA BOMBECK

Can you walk your talk?

Admittedly, keeping hope alive and refusing to be topped does not always lead to victory. However, refusing to be a quick quitter is one of the surest ways to shift the odds of success heavily in your favor.

A string of excited, fugitive, miscellaneous pleasures is not happiness; happiness resides in imaginative reflection and judgment, when the picture of one's life, or of human life, as it truly has been or is, satisfies the will, and is gladly accepted.

—GEORGE SANTAYANA

Responsible people do not blame circumstances, conditions, or conditioning for their behavior. Their behavior is a product of their own conscious choice.

—STEPHEN R. COVEY

If you find yourself stuck and
waiting for something to change,

WHY

NOT START

WITH

YOURSELF?

Are you
responsibility challenged?

When friends ask for a favor, do they usually bring
a contractual agreement or a waiver?

What you make of your life is
UP TO YOU

Every person creates his or her own reality. Authorship of your life is one of your absolute rights; yet so often people deny that they have the ability to script the life they desire. They look past the fundamental truth that it is not our external resources that determine our success or failure, but rather our own belief in ourselves and our willingness to create a life according to our highest aspirations.

103

There's nothing wrong with being realistic—as long as you

create your own reality.

—BETH MENDE CONNY

SUCCESS

I would challenge you to test the principle of proactivity for thirty days. Simply try it and see what happens. For thirty days work only in your Circle of Influence. Make small commitments and keep them. Be a light, not a judge. Be a model, not a critic. Be part of the solution, not part of the problem…When you make a mistake, admit it, correct it, and learn from it—immediately. Don't get into a blaming, accusing mode. Work on things you have control over. Work on you.

—STEPHEN R. COVEY, *The 7 Habits of Highly Effective People*

You do not need to be extraordinarily talented to succeed. All you really need is to discover work that you love and then **persist,**

persist,

persist.

That's the only secret.

If you look at things properly,
there's no need to wait for the dessert cart.
Dessert is
everywhere.

—MERRILL MARKOE

I don't know the key
to success, but the
key to failure is trying
to please everybody.

—BILL COSBY

How can you create your own momentum?

A wise woman who was traveling in the mountains found a precious stone in a stream. The next day she met another traveler who was hungry, and the wise woman opened her bag to share her food. The hungry traveler saw the precious stone and asked the woman to give it to him. She did so without hesitation. The traveler left, rejoicing in his good fortune. He knew the stone was worth enough to give him security for a lifetime. But a few days later, he came back to return the stone to the wise woman. "I've been thinking," he said, "I know how valuable the stone is, but I give it back in the hope that you can give me something even more precious. Give me what you have within you that enabled you to give me the stone."

—UNKNOWN

Successful people know fear—
but forge ahead anyway.

—HOLLY STIEL

Everyone needs recognition for his accomplishments but few people make the need known quite as clearly as the little boy who said to his father: "Let's play darts. I'll throw and you say

'Wonderful!'"

—*The Best of Bits and Pieces*

Success and failure are both greatly overrated.

But failure gives you a whole lot more to talk about.

—HILDEGARD KNEF

There is no point at which you can say, "Well, I'm successful now. I might as well take a nap."

—CARRIE FISHER

If someone was going to name something after you,

what would it be?

I have learned, as a rule of thumb, never to ask whether you can do something. Say, instead, that you are doing it. Then

fasten your seatbelt.

The most remarkable things follow.

—JULIA CAMERON

About Franklin Covey

Franklin Covey is the world's leading time management and life leadership company. Based on proven principles, our services and products are used by more than 15 million people worldwide. We work with a wide variety of clients, Fortune 500 material, as well as smaller companies, communities, and organizations. You may know us from our world-renowned Franklin Planner or any of our books in the 7 Habits series. By the way, Franklin Covey books have sold over 15 million copies worldwide—over $1\frac{1}{2}$ million each year. But what you may not know about Franklin Covey is we also offer leadership training, motivational workshops, personal coaching, audiotapes and videotapes, and *PRIORITIES* magazine just to name a few.

Let Us Know What You Think

We'd love to hear your suggestions or comments about *Choice: Choosing the Proactive Life You Want to Live*. And we'll let you know when the other books in The Portable 7 Habits series are available.

www.franklincovey.com/portable7

The Portable 7 Habits
Franklin Covey
MS0733-CK
2200 West Parkway Boulevard
Salt Lake City, Utah 84119-2331 USA

1-800-952-6839
International (801) 229-1333 Fax (801) 229-1233

RECOMMENDED READING

Allenbaugh, Eric, Ph.D. *Wake Up Calls: You Don't Have to Sleepwalk Through Your Life, Love, or Career!* Fireside, 1994.

Breathnach, Sarah Ban. *Something More: Excavating Your Authentic Self.* Warner Books, 1998.

Bunnell, Jean. *You Decide! Making Responsible Choices.* Instructional Fair, 1998.

Covey, Stephen R. *Living the 7 Habits: Stories of Courage and Inspiration.* Simon and Schuster, 1999.

———. *The 7 Habits of Highly Effective Families.* St. Martin's Press, 1998.

———. *The 7 Habits of Highly Effective People.* Simon and Schuster, 1989.

Hammond, John S. *Smart Choices: A Practical Guide to Making Better Decisions.* Harvard Business School Press, 1998.

Jeffers, Susan. *Feel the Fear and Do It Anyway.* Fawcett Books, 1992.

Kreeft, Peter. *Making Choices: Practical Wisdom for Everyday Moral Decisions.* Servant Publications, 1990.

Levoy, Gregg Michael. *Callings: Finding and Following an Authentic Life.* Three Rivers Press, 1998.

MacKenzie, Gordon. *Orbiting the Giant Hairball: A Corporate Fool's Guide to Surviving with Grace.* Viking Press, 1998.

Null, Gary. *Choosing Joy: Change Your Life for the Better.* Carroll & Graf, 1998.

O'Connell, Timothy E. *Good People, Tough Choices: Making the Right Decisions Every Day.* Thomas More Press, 1999.

Scott, Steve. *Simple Steps to Impossible Dreams: The Fifteen Power Secrets of the World's Most Successful People.* Simon & Schuster, 1998.

Sloan, Tod. *Life Choices: Understanding Dilemmas and Decisions.* Westview Press, 1996.

Stoddard, Alexandra. *Making Choices: Discover the Joy in Living the Life You Want to Lead.* Avon Books, 1995.

———. Making Choices: *The Joy of a Courageous Life.* William Morrow & Company, 1994.

Vanzant, Iyanla. *Yesterday I Cried: Celebrating the Lessons of Living and Loving.* Simon & Schuster, 1999.